Going Bananas

Watch for these
Shooting Star books:

Mystery of the Lunchbox Criminal
by Alison Lohans

Speedy Sam
by Dorothy Joan Harris

Some other books by
Budge Wilson:

The Best/Worst Christmas
Present Ever

A House Far from Home

Mystery Lights at Blue Harbour

Going Bananas

BUDGE WILSON

Illustrated by
Graham Pilsworth

Scholastic-TAB Publications Ltd.
123 Newkirk Road, Richmond Hill, Ontario Canada

Scholastic-TAB Publications Ltd.
123 Newkirk Road, Richmond Hill, Ontario, Canada L4C 3G5

Scholastic Inc.
730 Broadway, New York, NY 10003, USA

Ashton Scholastic Limited
165 Marua Road, Panmure, PO Box 12328, Aukland 6, New Zealand

Ashton Scholastic Pty Limited
PO Box 579, Gosford, NSW 2250, Australia

Scholastic Publications Ltd.
Holly Walk, Leamington Spa, Warwickshire CV32 4LS, England

Canadian Cataloguing in Publication Data
Wilson, Budge
Going bananas
(Shooting star)
Issued also in French under title: Ça suffit, les singeries!
ISBN 0-590-73365-6

I. Pilsworth, Graham, 1944- . II. Title.
III. Series.

PS8595.I58G6 1989 jC813'.54 C89-095215-9
PZ7.W55Go 1989

8 7 6 5 4 3 2 1 Printed in Canada 9/8 0 1 2 3 4/9
Manufactured by Webcom Limited

To my friend,
Marie Milton Davis

Contents

Chapter 1

A Pair of Nuts

Mrs. Dooley often said that her son Duff and his best friend, Simon Abrams, were a pair of nuts. Mrs. Abrams was fond of remarking that Duff and Simon were nice, but crazy.

Mr. Dooley seemed too worried about other things to have a great deal to say about the boys. But on the whole, he was good- natured about them. If Duff said, "Dad. There's an elephant in your bed," Mr. Dooley would just say, "Well, get him out, then. I'm tired, and want to get to sleep."

Over at the Abrams, things were pretty much the same. If Simon said, "Dad, today Duff and I hunted for dinosaurs all afternoon in Jackson Park," Mr. Abrams would just smile and say, "Is that so?"

Or at least he used to. Lately, he'd started to frown a little. It seemed to him that maybe the boys were getting a bit old for that kind of thing — that maybe they shouldn't be spending quite so much time making things up.

The fact is that Duff and Simon did spend a large part of each day hunting lions, walking on the moon, or killing dragons. These were perhaps strange occupations for two nine-year-old boys living in a small and ordinary city in North America. But Duff and Simon didn't think so.

It is true that they also did most of the other things that boys do. They played hockey on the neighbourhood rink in winter, and played baseball in Hastings Park in the summer. They liked to swim and to ride their bikes and to watch T.V. Often you would think they were just any old average kids.

But they weren't. Most of their free time was spent in the company of bats and wild cats, of magic spells and deadly laser beams, of men from Mars and hunters from Africa, of all kinds of weird beings that they dreamed up, played with, and talked about.

Duff and Simon gave names to all their creatures — Goliath, Winifred, Harry, Sylvester, Clementine. Duff had a favourite name that he was saving for a special person or animal or spirit or thing. The name was Mulligan. He didn't know why he liked it so much, but he did. And he wasn't going to use it until the time was right.

Needless to say, boys who spend their time in such amazing company often have pretty astonishing adventures. One day in the middle of winter, when Duff and Simon were killing giants in the school grounds after four o'clock, Duff suddenly yelled to Simon, "Watch out for that big one — the one called Harry!"

Then he shouted, "You're dead! Harry just

stepped on your head and crushed you like a mashed-up beetle. Fall down, Simon! Try to look like a burst tomato!"

So Simon dropped to the ground and tried to seem as squashed as possible. Duff ran over to him, shook him, and then let out a wild, ear-piercing shriek. "Simon!" he yelled. "My friend! My best and only friend! Dead! Dead! Dead!"

Over on Grandview Avenue, a lady looked out her front door and saw Simon lying on the ground. She also heard Duff's screams, and listened hard to what he was saying. Flapping her hands around in the air, she rushed to the phone, muttering, "Oh, dear heavens, dear heavens!" Then she phoned the police and the ambulance.

Soon the cold February air was filled with the sound of sirens, as a police car and an ambulance came wailing into the school grounds within seconds of one another. The men flew out of their vehicles, only to be greeted by two surprised and very healthy boys.

Later on, Duff said to his father, "Why were they so mad? Would they have liked it better if Simon had been really dead?"

His dad just sighed, and said, "Can't you and Simon do something *normal* for a change?"

When Simon saw the frowns on his parents' faces, he groaned. "Isn't *anybody* glad I'm alive?" he complained.

Chapter 2

Geronimo and the Lady

It's no wonder, then, that sometimes the Dooleys and the Abrams got tired of what Mrs. Dooley called "all that foolish nonsense" — of the way that Duff and Simon pretended themselves into all kinds of difficulties.

Like that sunny, warm day in late March when Simon was being a grizzly bear called Geronimo. Duff was pursuing him down the street with a water pistol, and Simon was baring his teeth and growling, loping along like a high-speed bear.

As they roared along, the boys didn't notice a very dignified lady coming around the corner of Reid and Charlotte Streets. She had beautiful yellow hair piled on top of her head, and she wore a little fur jacket over her swirling black skirt. The snow had melted on the sidewalks, and she'd left her boots at home. She was clicking along on a pair of purple shoes with very high heels.

She rounded the corner just as Geronimo came thundering along. He collided with her, right outside the Peterborough Clinic. But not before Duff had emptied his water pistol in Simon's direction, hitting not Simon, but the lady in the purple shoes.

She ended up on the sidewalk, with Simon sitting in her lap. She wasn't hurt, but her beautiful golden hair-do had come loose from its pins, and was tumbling all over her face and neck. And water was trickling down off her ear and into her little fur jacket.

"Odious boys!" she cried, as she picked herself up and brushed herself off. When Duff

handed her purse to her, she repeated (through her teeth), "Odious boys!" and disappeared into the Peterborough Clinic to find a washroom where she could repair the damage to her hair.

"Odious?" asked Simon. "What's it mean?"

"Dunno," said Duff. "We'll ask Dad."

It was a Saturday, and when they reached the Dooleys' house, Mr. Dooley was there. He was watching television and frowning. He had been frowning a lot lately. People were being laid off at work, and he kept wondering how long he was going to be able to keep his own job. He kept saying things to his wife, like, "How much did that meat cost?" or "Why are you buying cookies? It would be cheaper if you made them."

"Odious?" he repeated, when the boys asked him. "Why do you ask?"

"Because this lady said —" and here Duff stopped speaking.

"Said what?" His father looked stern. He switched off the T.V.

"Oh, just some silly thing," muttered Duff. "What's it mean?"

His father reached for the dictionary, and leafed through the pages, searching for the word. "Ah!" he said finally. "Here it is. It says, 'Odious — adjective. Hateful, repulsive.'" Mr. Dooley looked hard at Duff. "What else did she say, Duff?"

"Oh, not much," said Duff, staring at his fingernails and then scratching his red head. "It had to do with the bear." Then he jumped up. "Gotta feed the cats," he said, and rushed out of the living-room.

"Crazy!" exclaimed Mrs. Dooley, but she was smiling. Both of them shook their heads, and even Mr. Dooley chuckled.

That was before they knew anything about Mulligan-Chee-Chaw. That happened later on in the year, in May.

Chapter 3

Discovery!

It was May 12th. Duff lay in his bed and listened to the traffic on Clonsilla Avenue. It was early morning, but the night shift was ending, and some of the day workers were already on their way to the big Steel Plant. His father worked at the plant, so Duff knew where all those cars were going. A bus screeched to a stop half a block away, and he could hear men laughing, and the click of high heels.

It was almost time for Duff to get up. But in just six weeks time, the summer holidays would start, and then he wouldn't have to get up at exactly the same time every single morning. He might even want to get up earlier, because in the summer there are so many interesting things to do.

He and Simon could go over to Hastings Park and join the rest of the kids in a game of softball. They could play with their Frisbees, or wander around just talking, without anyone to tell them it was late or early or time to be somewhere else. They could go over to Jackson's Park and look for pirates hiding under the bridge, or search for discarded flying saucers or stray elephants in the picnic area.

Duff grinned when he thought about all the crazy things that he and Simon would dream up. Only yesterday, his father had said that he and Simon had too much imagination for their own good.

But today was a school day, and Duff jumped out of bed and put on his clothes — his jeans, his Adidas, and the red shirt that his mother said clashed with his hair. He could smell and hear bacon sizzling on the kitchen stove, and he was hungry. He raced down the narrow stairway and plopped himself down at the kitchen table.

"Ready," he announced to his mother, and held out his plate.

His mother came over and kissed him on the top of his untidy red hair. "Feed the cats first," she said. "And it wouldn't do your hair any harm if you put a comb through it."

Duff went out to the huge garage that had once been a barn when the city had been smaller. Long ago, their house had been a farmhouse, and sixty years ago there had been cows in the barn and chickens in the back yard. Duff liked to think about those days.

Duff opened the big door of the old barn and called the two cats, who often slept out there in the warm months. The barn was full of junk as well as lots of useful things, like his father's tools, and three bicycles, and a tire pump, and spare flower pots, and skis, and lawn chairs, and snow-shovels, and an old barbecue and a lawn-mower.

The only thing there didn't seem to be any room for was a car. But Mr. Dooley said their car was so old there was no use protecting it any more. "And," he added, "it'll be a long time before we can afford to buy a new one."

When the cats didn't come running to greet him, Duff began to look for them. Then he stopped as suddenly as if he'd been lassooed.

There was a monkey sitting on top of their old broken rocking chair.

Duff dashed back to the house. "Mom! Dad!" he yelled, "There's a monkey in the barn!"

"There he goes again!" laughed Mrs. Dooley, and his father smiled too.

"Elephants yesterday, monkeys today," he said. "And probably a gangster with a boa constrictor tomorrow." Then he looked more stern. "Duff. Hurry. Feed those cats and get back in here and eat your breakfast. School starts in fifteen minutes. Lucky for you it isn't far away."

Duff returned to the old barn. The monkey was still sitting on the rocking chair. "Hi,

monkey," whispered Duff, and then went and filled the cats' dishes with food, very quickly.

He put the dishes outside. Returning, he gazed at the monkey for a few long minutes, and then said, "Please, monkey. Be here when I get home from school. Please. I'll bring Simon. We'll give you a name, and we'll bring you some supper."

The monkey looked solemnly at Duff and scratched his chest and stomach. His long tail reached down to the floor. There was a large curve on the end of it. "Bye, monkey," said Duff, and left. He closed the door behind him very carefully.

When Duff got to the school yard, he called out to all the kids, "Hey, guys! Listen! Guess what! There's a monkey in our barn!"

"Gimme a break!" said one of the big boys in Grade 6. "That kid is something else. Last week he told us there was a sea serpent in Little Lake. Now it's a monkey in the barn."

"But there *is*. There *really* is!" insisted Duff. He went over to where Simon was hanging upside down on the jungle gym, and he told him the whole story. "After school," he whispered. "Over at my house. You'll see!"

Chapter 4

Simon Meets Mulligan

When school started that morning, Duff could hardly wait for Silent Reading period. He knew exactly which book he would choose. It was on top of the largest bookcase, and it was called *Jungle Animals and Their Way of Life*. He had to find out what monkeys ate, and this book would be able to tell him, for sure.

It did. "Monkeys eat tropical birds and tropical leaves and bananas." Well, bananas he could manage. He had eight dollars saved towards a new Titan hockey stick, and winter was a long way off. If the monkey stayed and lived in their barn forever, he would need more than eight dollars, but he wasn't going to worry about that just yet.

During Show and Tell, Duff tried again. "Mrs. Huppman," he began, "today I went out to feed the cats, and instead, I found a monkey in the barn."

"Duff," said Mrs. Huppman kindly, "you know the rules for Show and Tell as well as I do. You bring or you tell about real things. Keep your story until Story Time. Then you can write it all down or tell it. It might make a very interesting story about pretend things. Loretta, it's your turn. What have you brought?"

Loretta smiled happily and held up a huge curly-headed doll, made by hand and almost as big as she was. "Yesterday," she said, "my aunt came to visit us from Vancouver, and she brought me this!"

"Girls!" muttered Duff to Simon, who was sitting beside him. "Dolls! Wait'll they see this monkey! *That'll* open up their eyes!"

There was a Music Festival practice at noon, so all the kids had brought their lunches. Duff wasn't even hungry, and he wasn't sure he could live through the seven times they sang the same song over and over and over. However, he did live, and after a while it was three-thirty, and he could leave.

Duff and Simon dashed down to the Parkway Variety Store and bought some bananas. Then they set off for the Dooleys' house, running most of the way.

"What's in the bag?" asked Mrs. Dooley, as she finished spreading peanut butter on their sandwiches.

"Oh, you know," said Duff, between mouthfuls of bread. "Stuff for the monkey."

Mrs. Dooley was used to Duff's bags of stuff, and asked no more questions. Yesterday she had found a bag of stuff under his pillow. It had contained nine chestnuts, four speckled rocks, six huge bolts, two elastic bands, a pigeon feather, a padlock, nine pine cones, a magnifying glass, thirty-five hockey cards, and several pieces of chewing gum.

When Duff and Simon went out to the barn, the monkey was not on the rocking chair. "Aw, Duff!" complained Simon, who was still out of breath from racing most of the way up Sherbrooke Street. "I thought you really meant it this time."

"I did. I *did*!" snapped Duff crossly, searching on the shelves and above the skis, and behind the boxes of old pop bottles and jam jars. "Maybe he got hungry, and just up and left. He could probably figure out a way to get out through the old stove hole." Now, what the heck am I going to do with two dollars worth of bananas, he thought.

Suddenly Duff yelled, "*Mulligan*!" He had the name all ready.

There was the monkey, hanging by his long fingers from one of the high beams. Simon looked up. "Awesome!" he whispered. "*Awesome*!" He dropped his library book and baseball bat, and his mouth fell wide open.

Duff laid a banana down on the rocking chair.

Swinging from rafter to rafter, jumping on soft noiseless feet, Mulligan leapt down onto the chair and gobbled up the banana. Then he bounced up and down, squealing.

"I know exactly what he's saying," said Duff. "He's saying 'More! More! More!'" He gave Mulligan two more bananas, and then the boys stared at him as he ate them.

The monkey held the second banana daintily with the long, long, skinny fingers of one hand, and thoughtfully scratched his head with the other.

The boys spent the next hour watching the monkey leap, jump, scratch, mutter, and finally fall asleep on the old rocking chair. They were almost too excited to talk about it, even between themselves.

When they went back to the house, Duff's mother asked, "Where on earth have you two been for so long? It's almost supper time, and Mrs. Abrams has been calling and calling about Simon."

"Outside in the old barn, of course," said

Duff. "With the monkey."

"Yes, dear," said Mrs. Dooley, smiling. "Of course. In the barn with the monkey." Then she added, "And now off you go, Simon. I think your mom's a little bit worried."

Chapter 5

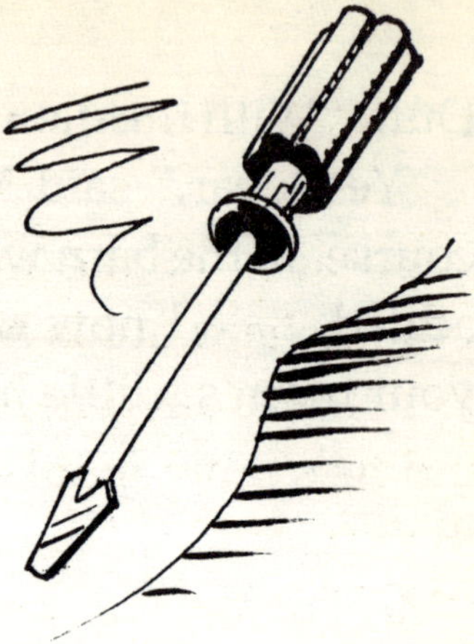

Fear in the Barn

That evening, after it was dark, Mr. Dooley came into Duff's room, where he was doing his homework. "Duff," he said, "will you please go get my screwdriver out of the barn?"

Duff paused a moment before answering. He thought about the dark old barn and Mulligan's beady little eyes. "Lookit, Dad," he said, "can I get it for you first thing in the morning?"

"But why?" asked his father. "I need it now. Right this minute. One of the light sockets is broken, and your mother needs the light for her sewing. Why not now?" Mr. Dooley was frowning.

"Because of the monkey," mumbled Duff, looking hard at his homework. "He's not a bit scary in the daytime, but it's really dark tonight, and he's a big monkey, and I don't know him all that well yet."

Mr. Dooley was not amused. "There may be a time and a place for your pirates and your monsters and your elephants and your space creatures," he said sharply. "Or your monkeys. But this isn't it. Out you go, young man, and bring that screwdriver right back."

Duff went. He coughed loudly as he entered the barn, so that Mulligan would hear him coming and not be frightened into doing something crazy, LIKE JUMPING DOWN ON HIS HEAD. He stamped his feet going across the floor to his father's work-bench, and then swung the flashlight around nervously until he found the screwdriver. Up above, he could hear low chattering noises.

Grabbing the screwdriver off the rack on the

wall, he ran towards the door as fast as he could go, tripping over the old rocking chair. He fell flat on his stomach, but he hardly even felt it.

Picking himself up, he slammed the door shut, ran the bolt through, and raced back to the house. He arrived in the kitchen panting, with his eyes large and round.

"See him?" asked his father, who was feeling friendly again.

"No," heaved Duff, "but I sure could hear him."

"Sure," said his father, and took the screwdriver.

"Thanks," he said.

Chapter 6

Problems

The next week was an exciting one for Duff and Simon. Every afternoon was spent in the barn, where they gradually made friends with Mulligan. The monkey was cheerful and intelligent, full of games and tricks and wonderful gymnastic leaps and swings. Duff and Simon talked about him constantly at home, at school, at play.

Duff's older sister Eileen would say, "Oh, sure. Whatever you say." The teacher would plead, "Oh, come now, Duff!" or *"Please,*

Simon!" Their friends kept saying, in tired voices, "Yeah. Yeah. Tell us another one."

Duff and Simon were having such a fun time that they didn't much mind that no one believed them. Besides, they were used to it. After all, they had told tall tales about seeing elephants stampeding in the school playground. And spacemen in Woolworth's. And rattlesnakes in the girls' locker room.

As time passed, however, Duff found that his life became more difficult. His mother started to be concerned about him.

His father became more and more impatient; he had enough to worry about without imaginary monkeys in his own barn. Duff's sister Eileen was embarrassed. She didn't like admitting to her friends that it was her brother who was "seeing monkeys."

Mrs. Dooley consulted the doctor, and asked him if he thought Duff was really and truly healthy and normal. She suggested that he be given tests. Mr. Dooley simply told his son that he didn't want to hear another single word about that monkey. Secretly, he went and talked to the priest at the church. What did you do when you found your son and his friend swinging from branch to branch in the old apple tree, pretending to be monkeys? What did you do, he asked, when that same son told lies all the time?

It was small wonder that no one believed Duff and Simon. Again and again, they took friends and family out to the barn to prove that the monkey was really and truly there. But unless the boys were alone, Mulligan hid in the rafters where no one could see him, and kept very, very quiet.

Peterborough, Ontario, is not exactly next door to the jungle. Even though half-eaten bananas and banana skins were often in the barn, even though there was a funny animal smell in the air sometimes, still no one believed them. After all, Sam Hoo Yung was the only kid in the class who had ever even *seen* a monkey, and that had been in the Metro Toronto Zoo, over 100 kilometres away.

At school, the kindly and patient Mrs. Huppman became impatient and less kindly. She didn't actually come right out and accuse Duff and Simon of lying, but she did say that if they didn't confine their stories to Story Time, she would speak to the principal.

The other children were less careful. After a while, when Duff or Simon started talking about Mulligan, they simply growled, "Oh, shut up! Boring! *Boring*!" Then they would go off and play floor hockey, and not ask them to be on any of the teams.

Little by little, therefore, Duff's monkey became a burden to the boys. They were fond of him, fed him, and played with him. They stood on their heads to entertain him. They learned to make chattering monkey noises. They hung upside down from the branches of the apple tree. But they stopped talking about him.

And they had a hard time keeping Mulligan fed properly. It got so they could hardly stand to look at a banana. The monkey had a terrible

appetite from all that exercise among the rafters, and both their allowances were spent on the day they got them. Duff knew that if his father were laid off, his allowance might stop completely. *Then what*?

They picked up old pop bottles in the park to make money. They robbed their piggy banks. And that wasn't all.

Duff had to spend a whole Saturday morning at the doctor's office having tests and answering questions. Simon's mother went to the synagogue half an hour early one week in order to speak to the rabbi; and the Dooleys' priest gave two homilies in a row on the wickedness of lying.

After three weeks, everyone was starting to get short-tempered — the Dooleys, Simon's parents, the teachers, the boys themselves — even Mulligan. It was as though some of the anxiety had rubbed off on him, too.

Most people were relieved, then, when they heard that the circus was coming to Peterborough. A circus is an event that most people enjoy — even doctors and priests and rabbis and teachers and parents. Besides, the two boys looked forward to seeing the Monkey Act. They thought they might learn some new tricks to teach Mulligan. It would be fun comparing their own monkey with the circus experts.

Of course, there was a lot of teasing from the other kids in school. "Tomorrow you'll be seeing some *real* monkeys, eh, Duff?" they said. And Mrs. Dooley said to her husband, "Maybe if he sees some monkeys at the circus, he'll stop pretending he can see a monkey in the barn. Oh dear. Let's hope so. It's really starting to get on my nerves."

Mr. Dooley said, "There, there, dear," and patted her knee. Secretly he thought, "This is one problem I just don't know how to solve. Drat that boy for worrying his mother!"

Chapter 7

Chee-Chaw

The circus was a great success. The night of the show was pleasant and warm, and the circus grounds were teeming with people happily munching on cotton candy and hot dogs.

Inside the enormous tent, the seats rose almost to the roof, and everyone seemed to be eating popcorn and laughing and shouting, waiting for the show to begin. Finally the bugles and drums announced the start of the performance, and the clowns came tumbling in, dressed in baggy pants and flapping shoes, their noses almost as big as their huge, painted grins.

The audience gasped and squealed as the trapeze lady flew through the air, catching the bar at just the right moment. Even old Mr. Jamieson, who was never impressed with anything, let out a gasp when she almost missed. Duff heard him.

Then the lions did their tricks, without gobbling up the trainer; and girls in pink jackets and skirts with gold fringes did terrifying things on the backs of racing white horses. The bears roller-skated and somersaulted, and the tightrope walker breezed across that rope as if it were as wide as a sidewalk. Only the steady dip-dip of his long balance bar showed the audience just how difficult a trick it was.

At last it was time for the Monkey Act. Duff's sister dug him in the ribs, and he and Simon leaned forward in their seats.

Out they marched — a little troupe of monkeys dressed in matching red coats, with tiny Mountie hats on their heads.

When they reached the centre of the ring, the trainer stood up on a stool. He had a shiny bald head and a huge black moustache. He bowed four times and raised his hand for silence.

Then, through his microphone, he made this announcement:

"Ladeez and gennulmen! We bring you now the famous Mountie Monkey Act. It will be good! It will be great! But I will have to warn you. There may be some very slight imperfections in the performance. Our lead monkey, Chee-Chaw, escaped from his cage when we were passing very close to Peterborough, near Omemee, three and a half weeks ago. He hasn't been seen since. The other monkeys depended on him for leadership. He was like a little monkey general."

Here the trainer took out a large, checkered handkerchief and wiped his eyes. Then he raised both arms and called out, "But the show must go on! They will do their best, and believe me, it will be good!"

Duff and Simon looked at one another.

Simon's black eyes were as round and as big as marbles. Mrs. Dooley looked at Mr. Dooley, and the two of them looked across the aisle at the Abrams. Over in the opposite bleachers, Mrs. Huppman looked at Mr. Huppman, and the principal looked at both of them. The priest looked at the rabbi, and the doctor looked at everyone. And all over the stands, children were looking at one another, mouths open, giant question marks in their eyes.

Meanwhile, the trainer stepped down from his pedestal, raised his small baton, and called out, "Showtime!" Nothing happened for a moment. The trainer yelled *"Showtime!"* again, and finally a monkey in a fancy gold-trimmed jacket dropped down from high in the tent rigging. The band started to play, and the monkeys marched forward to begin their act.

Afterwards, almost no one who knew Duff and Simon could remember one single thing about the Mountie Monkey Act. When the circus was over, Mr. Dooley turned to Duff and placed his hands gently on his shoulders.

"Listen, Duff," he said. "Listen carefully. This is very important. Is this monkey-business of yours one of your pretend tales? *Or do you really have a monkey in the barn*? I must know."

"Yes, Dad, I do," said Duff. "And I guess I know where he came from now. He didn't just drop out of the sky or arrive straight from Africa."

As people started leaving the building, many of them looked over to where Duff and Simon were standing — kids, teachers, the doctor, the priest, the rabbi. Some of them waved, and they smiled shyly, as though they felt ashamed of themselves.

Chapter 8

Mr Antonio's Thank You

The Dooleys and Abrams waited until most of the crowd had left the tent and gone to get their cars in the Memorial Centre parking lot. Then they all went down to the trailer that belonged to the monkey trainer, and knocked at the door.

The trainer was dressed in a long, red nightshirt, and he didn't look very pleased about being disturbed. He just grunted and frowned as he stared at them.

Mr. Dooley spoke first. "I'm sorry to bother

you at this hour," he said, "but we think we may have your missing monkey."

A broad smile changed the trainer's sleepy, cranky face into something happy and welcoming. "I can't believe it!" he exclaimed in a big loud voice, throwing open the door to the two families. "This three and a half weeks without Chee-Chaw has been like a nightmare for me. Two years I spend training that lead monkey — my little Chee-Chaw — and then — poof! He is gone in one night. Come in! Come in! I will make for you hot chocolate."

"Wait, wait," said Mr. Dooley. "Before we celebrate, I think we should go along to the barn and make sure we have the right monkey. After all, would a circus monkey be so shy that any time extra people came into the barn, he would hide, and not make a sound? Nobody here has seen him except the two boys."

"Ho, ho!" cried the happy trainer. "You do have my Chee-Chaw. I am sure of it now! Chee-Chaw is trained to stay hidden in the tent rigging in front of a crowd until I shout,

'Showtime!' — then he drops down for everyone to see. Like the silly monkey you saw today was supposed to. Only nobody is as good as my Chee-Chaw. Come, come with me, and I will show you." He hauled on a pair of trousers, and stuffed his nightshirt inside.

So all the Dooleys and Abrams went along to the Dooleys' barn, even though by now it was very dark.

When the trainer went into the barn with all the people behind him, he turned on the flashlight Mr. Dooley had handed him. The monkey was nowhere to be seen. Then he yelled, "Show- time!" and Chee-Chaw swung into view with a happy shriek and dropped down on the trainer's shoulder.

Then Mrs. Dooley invited everyone into the house for a little celebration party. Mr. and Mrs. Dooley and Eileen and Mr. and Mrs. Abrams said "I'm sorry" to Duff and Simon. Duff and Simon said "I'm sorry" to the trainer, whose name was Mr. Antonio.

He laughed. "Sorry!" he cried. "For what

should you be sorry? For looking after my little Chee-Chaw when he was lost, and feeding him many dollars worth of bananas in your nice safe barn? Besides, I don't mind being that miserable, now that it's all over. It was worth losing Chee-Chaw just to get him back." He let out a big laugh, and hugged his stomach.

Then he looked at the boys very hard. "Look," he said. "I want to do something really nice for you two boys, to say thank you from me and my Chee-Chaw. Think of something that is very wonderful, that you would like very much indeed."

The boys thought. They went to the end of the kitchen and talked together while the trainer drank hot chocolate with the Abrams and the Dooleys. Finally the boys returned and announced: "We've decided."

"What? What?" cried Mr. Antonio, clapping his hands. "Anything! Just tell me, and I will make it to happen before you can say one, two, three!"

Duff was the one to speak. "We'd like two free

tickets for tomorrow's performance, so that we can see Mulligan — no — Chee-Chaw in his act. But the second thing we want is harder. We want to keep Chee-Chaw long enough to take him to school tomorrow morning for Show and Tell. Can we?" Simon's black eyes were snapping. "*Can we?*" he pleaded.

"Can you!" boomed Mr. Antonio. "I should say you can! And I can do better than that. I'll bring two of my best monkeys along too, and give that class the best Show and Tell they ever saw!"

Then everyone said good night, and returned to their own homes.

But before they went to bed, the Dooleys all went out to the barn one last time. "Mulligan!" called Duff. "CHEE-CHAW! It's not showtime, but come down and meet my family anyway."

The monkey sailed down from the roof and landed squarely on the rocking chair. He looked around, scratched his chest thoughtfully, then shook hands with everybody.

"Oh, Duff!" said Mrs. Dooley, giving him a

big hug. "I feel so guilty about not believing you."

"Sorry, son," said Mr. Dooley.

"Me too!" said Eileen.

"That's O.K." said Duff. "With all the pirates and elephants and rattlesnakes around our house, I can see that you might have a real problem with Mulligan. But I'm sure glad it's all fixed up now." Then they all said good night to Mulligan-Chee-Chaw, and locked the barn for the night.

Chapter 9

Show and Tell

The next day, Mr. Antonio arrived very early in the morning. He brought the two other monkeys and a little Mountie suit with extra gold braid.

When Chee-Chaw saw him, he made happy welcoming noises, and rushed right over. Then Mr. Antonio dressed him in his pants and jacket and hat, and Duff drove with them to school, picking up Simon on the way.

They arrived at school ten minutes before the bell rang. Duff showed Mr. Antonio the First

Aid Room, and told him he wouldn't be disturbed until it was time for Show and Tell. Then he rushed off for roll call in his home room.

It seemed a long time to Duff and Simon before Show and Tell. After roll call, there was a Math class, and then they had a spelling test. Duff spelled twenty of the forty words wrong. After that, there was Silent Reading, and it was almost impossible to sit still. In fact, Simon got so fidgety that once he almost fell off his chair. Then came fifteen minutes of writing.

At last Mrs. Huppman said, "All right, class. Put your books in your desks and get ready for Show and Tell. If anyone wants first turn, raise your hand."

Duff's arm shot up like a rocket. "All right, Duff," said Mrs. Huppman. "When you've finished putting your books away, come up to the front of the room. When everyone is settled down, we'll start."

While all this was going on, Simon slipped out the rear classroom door, and raced down to the

First Aid Room. By the time Duff reached the teacher's desk, he could hear scuffles and squeaks out in the hall. Facing the class, he said, "I want you all to meet Mulligan, otherwise known as Chee-Chaw, and two of his friends." Then he opened the door.

While Mr. Antonio played a march on his harmonica, in came Mulligan-Chee-Chaw, followed by two other monkeys. They wore their red Mountie suits, and they did a fancy little step-hop as they entered the room. Every time Mulligan-Chee-Chaw did something new, the others did it too, right after him. They galloped all the way around the room as though they were riding horses. They leapt from desk to desk, and hung from the top edge of the blackboard. The kids laughed and laughed.

Mulligan jumped up on Mrs. Huppman's shoulder, and the other two monkeys did a little dance around her. She even got a case of the giggles.

The children clapped and clapped, and then the monkeys sat down at three of the empty

desks and clapped too. After a while, Mulligan-Chee-Chaw dashed over and sat in Duff's lap and gave him a hug. The other two monkeys went and sat on top of Simon's desk, and let him try on their hats and pat their heads.

Finally, Mr. Antonio passed around a giant bunch of bananas, and the class had a banana party.

Mrs. Huppman rose and called the class to order. "I think we all owe Duff and Simon an apology," she said. "For three whole weeks we haven't believed them about the monkey in the barn, and now we know that it was true. Duff — Simon — we're very sorry."

"Oh, that's O.K., Mrs. Huppman," grinned Duff. "I've thought about it a whole lot, and I decided that if anyone told me they had a monkey over at their house, I wouldn't believe it either. Especially if it was someone who was always talking about sea serpents and dragons."

Then it was Mr. Antonio's turn for a speech. "Now it is time for us to be going," he said. "I want to thank the boys for taking such good care of my Chee-Chaw. As a special thank you, I'm giving them a circus pass. That means they can go to the circus free, any time or anywhere we raise our big tent. Then they can see their old friend do his act whenever he is in a town near Peterborough.

"And to this great bunch of kids, I give an invitation. I want you all to come to the circus Saturday afternoon, free of charge, to see what a really great act our monkeys can perform, now that my Chee-Chaw is back to lead them."

The kids clapped and cheered, and then Mr. Antonio and his monkeys left.

Chapter 10

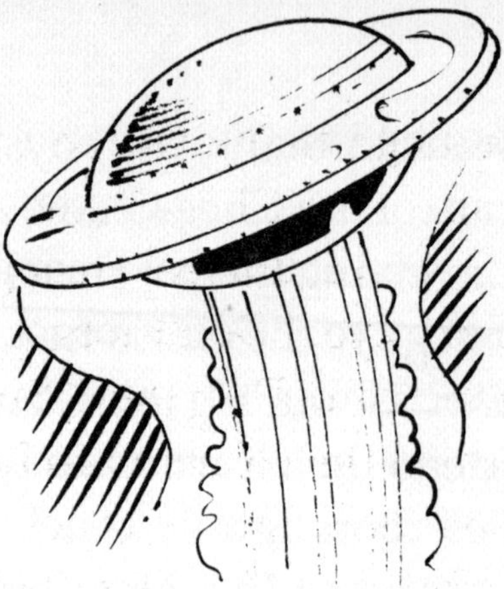

No More Monkey Business

After the performance on Saturday, Duff and Simon went into the animal tent to say goodbye to Mulligan-Chee-Chaw. Mr. Antonio let him out of his cage, and both Duff and Simon gave him a big hug.

They felt pretty sad to leave him, but they knew they would meet again. Duff gave him an extra large and perfect banana that he had stuffed in his pocket. "Have a nice summer, Mulligan-Chee- Chaw," he said, as the monkey was put back in his cage. "Thank you for coming to stay with us for a while. See ya next year."

Simon could feel a tear gathering in the corner of his eye. "Don't forget us," he whispered to Mulligan. Duff and Simon waved as they turned the corner onto Lansdowne Street, and the monkey waved back.

"Know what, Duff," sighed Simon, as they got closer to home, "I feel real bad. I feel like I've lost one of my best friends."

"Me too," said Duff, in a husky voice, as they turned up Sherbrooke Street from Monaghan Road. "One thing I know for sure. If we live to be a hundred and twenty years old, we'll never ever, as long as we live, have a real monkey in our barn again."

They walked up the street in silence for a while. Then Duff spoke. "The thing to do," he said, "is to think of something cheerful." They tried for a while, but couldn't come up with one single cheerful thing.

Duff picked up a rock and tried to hit a lamp post with it. "Missed," he said gloomily.

Simon kicked an old Coke tin along the sidewalk, till he stubbed his toe on a curb. "Ouch!" he howled, and then, "Who needs circuses and monkeys anyway!"

Then Duff started to look cheerful again. "What is it?" asked Simon, "Got an idea?"

"Well," began Duff, "I was thinking of all those circuses we're going to get to see. And for free. And of how famous we're going to be in school for a few days. And how it made me feel good right in the pit of my stomach to have all those people saying they were sorry. BUT."

"But what?" said Simon.

"Mostly," said Duff with a grin, as he shoved his fingers through his wild red hair, "I was thinking of what I'm going to do with my allowance this week."

"What?" asked Simon.

"SPEND IT!" shouted Duff, jumping over Mrs. Leblanc's garbage bag that she had left out for tomorrow's collection.

"AND NOT ON BANANAS!" yelled Simon.

"Right on!" said Duff. "Hey, Simon! Race you

home! Bet I can beat you four times over!"

"Bet you can't," hooted Simon, and away they both went up the hill.

"Hey, Simon," panted Duff, as they raced along, "how about spending the rest of the time before supper looking for stray spacemen who've fallen out of their saucers? O.K. by you?"

"O.K. by me!" said Simon.

And that's what they did.